SERMON OUTLINES
on

Practical Christian Living

Charles R. Wood

kregel
PUBLICATIONS

Grand Rapids, MI 49501

Sermon Outlines on Practical Christian Living

Copyright © 1999 by Charles R. Wood.

Published in by Kregel Publications, a division of Kregel, Inc., P.O. Box 2607, Grand Rapids, MI 49501. Kregel Publications provides trusted, biblical publications for Christian growth and service. Your comments and suggestions are valued.

Library of Congress Cataloging-in-Publication Data
Wood, Charles R. (Charles Robert), 1933–
    Sermon outlines on practical Christian living / Charles R. Wood.
        p.   cm. (Easy-to-use sermon outline series)
    Includes index.
    1. Prayer—Sermons—Outlines, syllabi, etc. 2. Christian life—Outlines, syllabi, etc. I. Title. II. Series: Wood, Charles R. (Charles Robert), 1933– Easy-to-use sermon outline series.
BV4223.W662   1999   251'.02—dc21   98-50467
                                                            CIP

ISBN 978-0-8254-4138-7

3 4 5 6 / 14 13 12

Printed in the United States of America

Introduction

Someone has said that the Bible is not a book of facts to be learned but rather a book of truths to be practiced. It is upon the truthfulness of this statement that the sermons in this book are based.

Practical Christian living is an increasingly popular subject among God's people. Many are weary of the routine, run-of-the-mill Christianity that merely conforms to the strictures and cultural norms handed down from previous generations. There appears to be a growing desire for freshness and practicality in applying biblical guidelines to life.

The sermons contained in this book have been created with the purpose of making it easy for the preacher to apply God's Word to the situations of everyday life. Real-life issues such as forgiveness, trials and temptations, materialism, procrastination, patience, and others are the primary subjects upon which the messages are built.

Each of the sermons included has been preached by the compiler of the book. This preaching has been to a medium-sized congregation that spans the gamut of social and economic classes, and is located in middle-America. And this preaching has been done within the past five years, so the messages are all contemporary attempts to speak creatively to the needs of the world in which we live.

As is always true of sermon outlines of this nature, these messages are designed to be preached after some period of personal preparation. Careful reading of the context, consultation with a commentary (many good single-volume commentaries are available today), and a prayerful period of reflective consideration will add flesh to the bare bones of an outline.

It has been said that a life lived according to the specific, practical teaching of the Word of God will never be one without challenge or reward. The truthfulness of this statement has been proven over and over again in the personal experience of the compiler of this collection. It has also been rewarding to see the benefits obvious in the lives of those to whom the sermons were originally delivered.

This book is presented with the sincere hope that the God who spoke in practical terms to humankind will use these sermons to produce practical changes in the lives of those who know and love Him.

Charles R. Wood

Contents

A New Way

Joshua 3:4

Introduction:
Israel faced an unknown situation in this story. Here are seven pointers for facing uncertainty:

I. **Face It Calmly**
    A. Israel didn't know the direction—they had to take things one step at a time
    B. We can be sure of certain things that produce calm
        1. We are heading in the right direction
        2. Our way has been safe up to this point
        3. Any fear, panic, etc. will not change the future

II. **Face It Submissively**
    A. This was a way chosen for Israel by their God
    B. If you are a child of God, this is not a way of your own appointing
        1. Change what you are reasonably able to change
        2. Accept as from Him the things that you can't change
        3. Stop trying to keep yourself in the love of God—you can't

III. **Face It Compliantly**
    A. This chapter is filled with commandments as was the entire conquest
    B. Hearing and heeding are two ways of facing the unknown
        1. We have all the instruction that we could possibly need
        2. We must resolve to hear the Word of the Lord and to do it

IV. **Face It Expectantly**
    A. God had good things in store for Israel
    B. God has good things in store for you
        1. You will experience the presence of the Lord
        2. The greater the trials, the greater the working of the Lord
        3. Even if there are new trials, they will likely end old trials

V. **Face It Confidently**
    A. Israel had the assurance of God's presence and power

       1. Note the role of the ark
       2. Note the new arrangement with the ark first—God didn't need them to protect Him; He was committed to protecting them
  B. Some things to remember
       1. The way is new to you, but not to your God—past, present, and future are all human words
       2. The way is new to you, but others have faced what you will face
       3. The presence of God goes with you more surely than with them

VI. Face It Aggressively
  A. Israel was facing enormous changes at this point
       1. They were not a warlike people—they had been in servitude and then itinerant
       2. They should have known conquest rather than wilderness wanderings
  B. Your way—if it involves growth—requires change
       1. Whatever will come is ordered by the Lord for your growth
       2. Take the way one step at a time, trusting the Lord

VII. Face It Cheerfully
  A. Israel didn't achieve on this point
       1. They should have been glad to get out of the wilderness
       2. They should have been glad to get on with conquest
  B. Face the year with some assurances
       1. Your difficulties will all be overcome or
       2. You will be given strength to handle trials
       3. "This is the day [way] the Lord hath made. . . ."

Conclusion:

Israel was commanded to "sanctify themselves"—make themselves holy. The best way we can approach any uncertainty is by recommitting ourselves to Him and His Word.

Dealing with Discouragement

1 Kings 19:1–19

Introduction:

Most of us are not strangers to discouragement. Most of us have known times when our discouragement actually turned into despair. "The main trouble with despair is that it is self-fulfilling. People who fear the worst tend to invite it." Elijah went through a period of discouragement, despair, and depression. There is much we can learn from him.

I. **The Causes of Discouragement**
    A. Emotional stress
        1. He had just been through incredible confrontation
        2. He was facing continuing problems
    B. Physical exhaustion
        1. He had run from before Jezebel (v. 3)
        2. He had gone even beyond that (v. 4)
    C. Personal opposition
        1. Jezebel had made threats (v. 2)
        2. He was actually in danger
    D. Significant achievement (18:42–45)
        1. He had just seen a great victory
        2. Discouragement often comes after triumph
    E. Basic fear (v. 2)
        1. He was afraid of what Jezebel could/would do to him
        2. Fear is a powerful emotion and it is usually negative
    F. Simplistic thinking
        1. He evidently thought that a victory would care for everything
        2. This made him vulnerable to despair's cousin, disillusionment
    G. Heavy responsibility (v. 10)
        1. The situation was clouded by his own misperception
        2. He saw himself as incredibly responsible

II. **The Process of Discouragement**
    A. Flight—he had run away from the trial
    B. Negative thinking—his words drip with negativity each time he speaks (vv. 4, 10)
    C. Withdrawal—he withdrew from men (vv. 4, 9) and actually appears to be withdrawing from God

D. Blame shifting (v. 10)—he laid the blame on the children of Israel and saw his problem as that of someone else
E. Improper comparisons (vv. 4, 10)—"Look what happened to my fathers, and I'm no better than they"

III. The Results of Discouragement
A. Personal isolation—through all of this he is alone
B. Loss of perspective (v. 10)—"I am the only one left"—he was not!
C. Self-pity—"Self-pity is a narcotic that leaves its addicts wasted and derelict"
D. Suicidal tendencies (v. 4)—he really didn't want to die, he just thought about it (if he had wanted to die, he could have stayed were he was, and Jezebel would have taken care of it)

IV. The Cure for Discouragement
A. Get up—physically (vv. 5, 7)—this was only after rest was granted—"Sometimes the most spiritual thing you can do is take a nap"
B. Look up—spiritually (vv. 11–14)—God came and spoke to him and gave him a message of hope
C. Link up—emotionally (vv. 16, 19a)—God gave him Elisha to strengthen him
D. Gird up—practically (vv. 15–17)—God gave him a job to do—it is easier to do your way into feeling than it is to feel your way into doing
E. Shape up—volitionally (v. 14)—Elijah still complains even after seeing God's glory, but God laid tasks before him—the choice was his

Conclusion:
"Despair is not handled by giving in. It is handled best by giving out something of yourself to others. By giving out a person has no time for despair, so it departs."

Patience and Fortitude
Psalm 27:13–14

Introduction:

Spurgeon said, "The Christian life is no child's play. All who have gone on pilgrimage to the celestial city have found a rough road, sloughs of despondancy and hills of difficulty, giants to fight and tempters to shun."

I. **Typical Trials**
   A. We don't have any idea when this Psalm was written
      1. It obviously refers to trials or was written in a time of trial
      2. David went through many trials—this may be a typical one
      3. This may be recorded in 1 Samuel 21:1–10 or in 1 Samuel 22:6–23
   B. What were some of the things typical of David's trials?
      1. Danger—Saul was plain on wanting to kill him
      2. Distress—personal anguish over the death of the priests
      3. Discomfort—his whole personal life was torn up
      4. Despair—he had little idea of the future

II. **Timeless Teaching**
   A. The encouragement of expectation (v. 13)
      1. He yet expected to see the goodness of the Lord
      2. He expected to see it in the "land of the living"—refers to this life here on earth
   B. The power of patience—"Wait on the Lord"—the hardest thing to do is nothing: "Sometimes the servant will have to wait in absolute inaction, and this is not always to the taste of energetic minds"
      1. Look to Him as your source—nothing comes other than from Him
      2. Stand before Him in submission
      3. Be patient for His timing—this is at the heart of so much!
      4. Stay in constant communion with Him
      5. Hold on to the things you believe: "Don't doubt in the dark what God has given you in the light"
   C. The factor of fortitude—"Be of good courage" (Courage: a state of mind which results from a decision of will)

1. Continue waiting on the Lord
2. Keep on facing life
3. Stay involved in service
4. Keep doing right
5. Remain faithful in prayer
D. The enhancement of experience—"And again I say"
   1. David adds his own experience here
   2. No matter when this was written, he had already been through more than most of us will ever face

III. Timely Truth
A. Things that are not promised:
   1. He will remove your trials
   2. He will remove you from trials
   3. He will make your life easy
B. The thing that is promised: He will strengthen your heart
   1. He will keep you in the trial
   2. He will keep you through the trial
   3. He will be a refuge in the trial
   4. He will use the trial

Conclusion:

Wait on the Lord. Stick around, be what you should be, do what you should do. As you do it, He will enable you to do it. Ultimately there will be a solution. "Hands off there, and leave it with the Most High!"

A Penny for Your Thoughts

Proverbs 4:23

Introduction:

This is often said when someone is deep in thought, but your thoughts are worth far more than a penny. In fact, your thoughts are among your most precious treasures. Solomon said, "For as he thinketh in his heart, so is he" (Prov. 23:7), and he likely knew more than you dream about the subject.

I. **What It Is That We Are to Do: "Keep thy heart . . ."**
   A. Any meaningful consideration of the heart must pass through the thoughts
      1. There is more to man than brain, but brains (thoughts) are what make the inner man meaningful
      2. Your thinking is what you really are
   B. Keeping the heart involves two things:
      1. What you allow to enter it
      2. What you allow to go on in it

II. **How We Are to Do It: "with all diligence"**
   A. With extreme care
      1. Not only diligence, but all diligence
      2. "Exercising the utmost care over . . ."
   B. "Above all other things you keep, . . ."
      1. If you kept your body like you keep your mind . . .
      2. If you kept your house like you keep your mind . . .
      3. If you kept your person like you keep your mind . . .
      4. If you kept your investments like you keep your mind . . .

III. **Why We Are to Do It: "for out of it are the issues of life . . ."**
   A. Because the mind does not naturally turn toward God
      1. It is deceitful (Jer. 17:9; Prov. 28:26)
      2. Its desires are determined by pride (Rom. 12:3)
   B. Because the mind determines what we are (Prov. 23:7)
      1. The real nature of a person is in his or her thoughts
      2. This is why a brain transplant is impossible
   C. Because the mind determines what we do
      1. Christ is very explicit on this (Matt. 12:35)
      2. This works in both directions (Dan. 5:6)
   D. Because we can sin with our thoughts
      1. Christ taught this (Matt. 5:28)
      2. There is infinitely more mental sin than physical

E. Because the mind is the correspondence point with temptation
    1. This is clearly taught in James 1:14
    2. This is the reason for Christ suggesting prayer (Mark 14:38)
F. Because uncontrolled thoughts lead to problems
    1. A controlled thought life is necessary to positive Christian living (2 Cor. 10:5)
    2. Uncontrolled thoughts can impact others (Heb. 12:15)
G. Because our desires arise out of our thoughts
    1. The "fruit of their thoughts" (Jer. 6:19)
    2. Very few sins are genuinely unpremeditated

Conclusion:

What you think about is incredibly important: revenge, bitterness, lust, hatred, discontent, pride, unreality untruth, etc. The ways in which you think are also incredibly important: negativity, worry, fantasies, brooding, self-pity, distrust, unhappiness, etc. Never take "a penny for your thoughts" as they are worth infinitely more than that. They can make you or break you spiritually.

Dog-eared

Proverbs 26:17

Introduction:

There is a well-known story about the late Lyndon Johnson holding his dogs by the ears and thus agitating animal lovers. Many Christians become involved in something similar, and it is the result of meddling in the affairs of others. This passage describes the situation.

I. **What Is Meddling?**
    A. The passage explains itself
        1. "Meddleth"—become inflamed, agitated about something
        2. "With strife"—describes a situation of contention
        3. "He that passeth by"—someone who is not on the scene, not a witness to what caused the strife
        4. "Belonging not to him"—the person has no personal stake in what has happened
    B. Can be expressed various ways:
        1. "He that interests himself in quarrels he has no business with"
        2. "Strive not in a matter that concerns thee not" (Greek proverb)

II. **What Are the Results of Meddling?**
    A. "Is like one that taketh a dog by the ears"
        1. This is not a wise way to handle dogs
        2. It seems to deal with the idea of a stray dog
        3. Doing so will rouse a dog's fury and expose one's self to savage bites
    B. A meddler exposes himself to danger
        1. "The man who becomes partisan in a quarrel that does not concern him renders himself liable to the anger of one, if not of both, of the contending parties"
        2. Once we are in strife that is not ours, it is difficult to get out
        3. Involvement in the strife of others almost always results in hurt
        4. Uninvited intervention rarely avails with the contending parties

III. **How Does Meddling Differ from Peacemaking?**
   A. There is a clear difference
      1. Peacemaking: neutrally seeking to bring parties together
      2. Meddling: siding with a party and seeking vindication
   B. Here are two guidelines
      1. Peacemaking is best done reluctantly and hesitantly
      2. We should be very sure of our call to act before we do so

IV. **Are There Biblical Illustrations Regarding Meddling?**
   A. The story of Jehoshaphat in 1 Kings 22
      1. Jehoshaphat is in a battle that was not his concern
      2. He escaped, but he very nearly lost his life for his trouble
   B. The incident in Luke 12:13–14
      1. Christ was confronted by a man who wanted Him to become involved in a quarrel
      2. Christ perfectly practiced Proverbs 26:17 at this point
      3. We would do well to pattern after Christ and avoid strife

V. **What Are the Lessons to Be Learned from Meddling?**
   A. "It is foolish to quarrel about our own concerns; it is the height of folly to become involved in things that don't concern us"
   B. "If we are not to be hasty to strive in our own cause [see Prov. 25:8], how much less in others, especially those in which we are in no way related or concerned"
   C. When we do intervene (as a peacemaker) we will do so after much prayer, with good reason and on the basis of solid biblical support

VI. **What Is the Answer to Meddling?**
   A. Recognize our natural tendency to it
   B. Accept biblical cautions against it (see 1 Peter 4:15–16)
   C. Heed the words of Paul: 1 Thessalonians 4:11 ("He who is not usefully occupied in doing his own business will be very apt to interfere impertinently with the concerns of others.")

Conclusion:
   We have forgotten God in our modern day. He is quite able to handle many things we want to handle. Beware of becoming dog-eared!

Renewal

Isaiah 40:31

Introduction:
"Human strength is of many kinds, but in any form it will spend itself in due time."

I. **The Need of Renewal**
   - A. Some have quit running
     1. They may still be around the race course
     2. They may still even be standing among the runners
   - B. Some are tired of running
     1. The race has been long and the course is difficult
     2. These are people who are contemplating quitting
   - C. Some are tired in running
     1. They are still plodding on
     2. They are tired and thus less effective in running
   - D. Just about everyone needs periodic renewal

II. **The Source of Renewal**
   - A. Resolution will not do
     1. It is good to make resolutions
     2. Resolution alone will not care for this problem
   - B. Self-help methods will not do
     1. This is the big stress today—you can do whatever you set out to do
     2. Many are finding that the race is too stringent for this
   - C. Only spiritual renewal will do
     1. The difficulties we face have a spiritual aspect
     2. Only a spiritual infusion will help
   - D. The Lord is the source of our strength

III. **The Manner of Renewal: "Wait on the Lord"**
   - A. It requires submission to His will
     1. We wait as a servant waits for instruction
     2. Only a submitted will waits
   - B. It requires listening to His Word
     1. There is no sure way to hear His voice outside His Word
     2. There is no way to wait on Him without listening for His voice
   - C. It requires obedience to His commands
     1. Submission settles the issue
     2. Continual commitment is required

D. It is only as we wait on the Lord that we will find strength

IV. The Results of Renewal
A. Help for the routine
1. "They shall walk and not faint"
2. The routine is the very most difficult of all
B. Strength for the extra demands
1. "They shall run and not be weary"
2. Ministry is extra demanding—a lot of work for few people; a lot of need for a few suppliers
C. Ability for the exceptional opportunity
1. "They shall mount up with wings as eagles"
2. We always have an incredible, exceptional opportunity before us

Conclusion:

"A church that is waiting on the Lord always knows where its strength lies, namely, in its God."

Great Expectations!

Matthew 5:47

Introduction:

God obviously expects more from His own people. There are "great expectations" for God's people.

I. **Why Are There Such High Expectations?**

"There are legitimate reasons why the world, the church, and our Lord Jesus Christ Himself, may expect more from Christians than from the rest of mankind."

   A. Christians profess more
      1. We claim to be something more than the world
      2. We often claim to be more than other Christians
   B. Christians are more
      1. We have been changed by the power of God
      2. We are now Sons of God and joint heirs with Christ
   C. Christians possess more
      1. We have the internal presence of the Holy Spirit
      2. We have the resources of prayer, etc.
   D. Christians promise more
      1. We have great potential in Him
      2. We "can do all things"
   E. Christians know more
      1. We have the Word of God to instruct us
      2. We understand so much more about life, the world, etc.
   F. Christians expect more
      1. We expect things from God; why not He from us?
      2. We expect things of other Christians; why not of ourselves?

II. **What Are These Expectations?**

Many of these high expectations can be found in the chapter in which this verse appears:

   A. Example (vv. 13–16)
   B. Obedience (vv. 17–20)
   C. Gentleness (vv. 21–26)
   D. Purity (vv. 27–32)
   E. Truthfulness (vv. 33–37)
   F. Patience (vv. 38–42)
   G. Love (vv. 43–48)

III. **Why Should I Meet These Expectations?**
There are very good reasons why God's people ought to measure up to high expectations:
   A. Because I am known by my fruits
      1. People should not judge, but they will
      2. There should be a differentness about Christians
   B. Because my works will be revealed
      1. Don't worry about not judging—He'll take care of it
      2. This is a matter of motives
   C. Because I can stop the talk of the enemy
      1. I can't stop all criticism, but I should not create any
      2. A godly life does silence the critic
   D. Because doing so will glorify God
      1. The more things are "out of character," the more they glorify
      2. I glorify God most by becoming like Him
   E. Because it brings peace to my own conscience
      1. I know I am doing what is right
      2. I know that I am doing what pleases the Lord

Conclusion:
   How we live is of significance. "The salvation of Christ is not in sin but from sin."

First Things First
Matthew 6:25–34

Introduction:

> The world is too much with us; late and soon,
> Getting and spending, we lay waste our powers:
> Little we see in nature that is ours;
> We have given our hearts away, a sordid boon!

The theme: worry, fret, care, concern, anxiety, etc.

I. **The Commandment**
  A. "Take no thought"
    1. It does not mean "be unmindful of"
    2. It rather means "don't be anxious or worried"
  B. Areas of concern:
    1. Life—life in general (v. 25)
    2. The details of life—food, raiment (v. 25)
    3. The duration of life—tomorrow and all it holds (v. 34)

II. **The Conditions**
  A. There are more important issues—than what you worry about (v. 25b)
  B. God cares for His animate creation—He won't care for you? (v. 26)
  C. God cares for His inanimate creation—likewise? (vv. 28–30)
  D. Worry doesn't change anything—what have you changed by worrying? (v. 27)
  E. Worry is the work of the heathen—any old sinner can worry (v. 32)
  F. Your Father already knows your needs—He already knew them before they developed into needs (v. 32b)
  G. Tomorrow will care for itself—each day has enough evil for that day, including today (v. 34)

III. **The Correction**
  A. "Seek ye"—keep being absorbed with serious effort
  B. "First"
    1. Chronologically
    2. In priority
    3. In intensity
  C. "The kingdom and righteousness of God"
    1. Kingdom: extend His rule outwardly
    2. Righteousness: expand His likeness inwardly

D. "Things shall be added"—what you seek for will come without the worry
E. "All these things"—all the details of life

IV. The Challenge
A. Replace worry with spiritual action
B. Realize that how you seek it is how you get it
C. Face the difficult decisions
   1. How do you put His kingdom and righteousness first?
   2. How have you done so this week?
D. Don't blame God for your worry or for your lack

Conclusion:
We're told not to fret! We're given good reasons not to do so! We're told how to avoid it! Get busy for God. Put the things of God first. If you are fretting, you are likely not busy for God!

Here Comes the Judge

Matthew 7:1f.; John 7:24

Introduction:

We are very good at what we are commanded not to do; we are very poor at what we are commanded to do. "There is a little of the Pharisee in every Christian."

I. **Let's Get Basic**
   A. Judge: To form a judgment based on opinion
   B. Discern: To tell the difference based on facts

II. **Let's Get Real**
   A. It is often necessary to judge in order to discern
      1. Note verses 6 and 15
      2. Note the meaning of 7:24
   B. It is almost impossible to avoid judging
      1. We are constantly called upon to make judgments
      2. It is almost as if Christ is giving us criteria for times when we must do so

III. **Let's Get Practical**
   A. The problem: harshly condemning others while passing over one's own faults
      1. Speaking about matters that are not our concern
      2. Putting prejudice in place of principle
      3. Putting personalities in place of principle
      4. Offering opinions not based on knowledge
      5. Passing judgment without considering circumstances
      6. Expressing opinions on motives
      7. Expressing judgments without indicating that they are such
   B. Judging can be very dangerous
      1. It can get you judged—both by God and man (vv. 1b–2)
      2. It can make you look foolish (vv. 3–5)
      3. It can be revealing—we tend to see our own problems reflected in others
      4. It can make you unlike God

IV. **Let's Get Biblical**
   A. We must eliminate:
      1. Censoriousness: harsh judgment without mitigation
      2. Harshness

3. Self-righteousness
4. Lack of mercy (see Luke 6:36)
5. Lack of love (see 1 Cor. 13)
B. If you must judge, do so
   1. Reluctantly
   2. Slowly
   3. Humbly
   4. After self-examination
   5. For a reason
C. We live in a mixed up Christian world
   1. What we think of ourselves is stressed but not important
   2. What we think of others is emphasized but less important
   3. What God thinks of us is ignored but truly significant

Conclusion:
Some fine lines are drawn by a passage such as this: We are not to judge, but we are to discern, which usually requires something very close to judgment. If we would see the whole picture here that Christ draws, we really wouldn't have a big problem with the matter.

Attitude and Altitude

Romans 12:3

Introduction:

There are two instruments on a plane's panel—one measures altitude, the other attitude. There are no instruments, but there are the same two attributes in life: 1) altitude has to do with the height of self-measure; 2) attitude has to do with one's general approach to life. Generally speaking, the higher the altitude, the worse the attitude.

I. **The Meaning of the Passage**
   A. It is often misinterpreted and misapplied
      1. It is used to support the "importance of self-esteem"
      2. The stress is on "than he ought to think"
   B. The obvious meaning is opposite
      1. The stress on "not to think more highly"
      2. This message comes with strong support from other Scripture
   C. Each of us is to think "soberly"
      1. This involves careful, thoughtful evaluations
      2. We must recognize that God has given us what we have
   D. General biblical teaching
      1. Pride is a major problem—it led to the fall of Satan and of man
      2. By nature we tend to think too highly of ourselves

II. **The Message of the Passage**
   A. A strong caution against pride, elevated opinion of self
   B. Pride has serious negative effects on us
      1. It affects our thinking
      2. It influences our performance
      3. It conditions our relationships
      4. It limits our spirituality
   C. Pride produces sins of the spirit: bitterness, unforgiveness, judgmentalism, desire for vengeance, irritability, anger, arrogance, hatred, envy, jealousy, covetousness, etc.
   D. If we are going to discover the will of God, we must deal with pride

III. **The Method of the Passage: How can I get a proper view of myself?**
   A. I am a serious sinner—if no one else had ever sinned, my sin alone would require Calvary

B. I am a potential disaster—I am capable of doing some very foolish things apart from the grace of God
C. I am constantly threatened—I am always on the brink of falling into sin
D. I am totally impotent—the only meaningful epitaph: "only a sinner saved by grace"
E. I am ultimately indebted—the only thing I have of real value is my salvation, which is totally a gift from Him
F. I am completely dependent—everything I have, including those things that I have earned with my hands or my brain, traces back to Him, to a gift from God
G. I am utterly equal—I am no better than anyone else—there are people of far lower status than I who are my superiors in character, etc.
H. I am incorrigibly human—I am infinitely inferior to God even though my thoughts and actions would seem to demonstrate at times that I believe I am superior to Him
I. I am significantly self-deceived—I have weaknesses and shortcomings that are evident to everyone but me
J. I am fortunately unexposed—there are things in my life that, were everyone to know them, would humiliate me

Conclusion:

There is nothing more loathsome to a proud heart than someone condemning pride. Coming to terms with what we really are, however, is a very liberating experience. Paul says, "Don't think of yourself more highly than you ought to think. Instead, think seriously and recognize that every worthwhile thing you have comes from the Lord."

How to Cram for a Daily Exam
1 Corinthians 10:13

Introduction:
Life includes a daily examination and this "testing" comes in two forms: 1) Trials (suffering internally, from others, over others) are allowed by God to test our Christianity. 2) Temptations (external solicitations to evil with internal correspondence) are brought by Satan to test our character. Testing is a daily matter and certain truths can help us face it.

I. **"God Is Faithful"**
    A. This is an absolute constant (2 Tim. 2:13)
    B. The alternative is unthinkable

II. **Your Testing Is "Common to Man"**
    A. It is a "man kind of testing"—not suited to angels, etc.
    B. It is not wrong to be tested (either tried or tempted)
    C. Others have been tested and have triumphed or resisted

III. **Your Testing Is Not Necessarily of Your Own Making**
    A. "Taken"—to seize, lay hold of, come upon
    B. Many trials are the result of the actions of others
    C. Temptations have a human element, but they originate with Satan

IV. **You Will Not Be Tested Beyond Your Ability**
    A. Testings are "tailor made" to each individual
    B. You can be sure
        1. The period won't be too long
        2. The number of tests won't be too great
        3. The weight of testing won't be excessive
        4. The power of the testing won't be overwhelming
    C. "I can't take any more" is either a wrong statement or one won't have to

V. **Some Means of Escape Will Accompany the Testing**
    A. There is a proper way to escape—a way provided by God
    B. The possible ways of escape may widely vary
    C. Most testings would be more bearable if we were looking for the way out rather than bemoaning the test.

VI. You Will Be Able to Bear It
A. A simple statement of fact
B. No one can claim freedom from obligation to "pass the course"—"spiritual maturity is not devastated by adversity"
C. Collapse or destruction is always a matter of choice

VII. We Have a Vast Set of Examples to Help
A. The context speaks of Israel (vv. 1–10)
1. They had God's guidance
2. They brought trouble on themselves
3. The nation was punished but still survived
B. We have other biblical examples of those who were tried yet survived
C. This is part of the "so great a cloud of witnesses"—check into Hebrews 11

Conclusion:
Tests are so constant that every day is a test in itself. Tests are designed for our good and spiritual development (even when they are the result of our own foolishness). We are expected to pass the tests of life.

The Thoughts and Actions of Love
1 Corinthians 13:4–7

Introduction:
Love: an intertwined combination of thoughts, feelings, and actions. Note the characteristics listed by Paul in 1 Corinthians 13. These things tell us what love is by the ways in which it acts.

I. **"Suffereth Long": it is "long-minded"**
   A. It means to be patient
   B. It is slow to take offense, react

II. **"Is Kind": it is "disposed to be useful to others"**
   A. It is good-natured
   B. It wishes others well

III. **"Envieth Not"**
   A. It doesn't begrudge anyone anything
   B. It doesn't feel badly over another's prosperity

IV. **"Vaunteth Not Itself": it "does not seek to win admiration or applause"**
   A. It eschews such things as boasting, bragging
   B. It never taunts

V. **"Is Not Puffed Up"**
   A. "A mind swelled with its own importance"
   B. This is simply conceit

VI. **"Doth Not Behave Itself Unseemly"**
   A. It is neither rude nor crude
   B. It does nothing of which to be ashamed

VII. **"Seeketh Not Her Own"**
   A. It is not selfish or self-centered
   B. It does nothing for personal interest

VIII. **"Is Not Easily Provoked"**
   A. It is not irritable or easily angered
   B. It is not quick-tempered

IX. **"Thinketh No Evil"**
   A. It does not keep track of evil
   B. "It keeps no record of wrong" (NASB)

X. **"Rejoiceth Not in Iniquity"**
   A. It is not glad about evil
   B. It never finds reason to be vindictive

XI. **"Rejoiceth in the Truth"**
    A. It gets excited about the good
    B. It becomes involved in spreading the gospel

XII. **"Beareth All Things"**
    A. This means "to cover with silence"
    B. It always seeks to protect—based on truth

XIII. **"Believeth All Things"**
    A. It tries to put things in the best light possible
    B. It is not suspicious

XIV. **"Hopeth All Things"**
    A. It always trusts things will work out for the best
    B. It lives looking for the silver lining

XV. **"Endureth All Things"**
    A. It always perseveres
    B. It hangs in against all odds

Conclusion:

We are commanded to love one another. These are the specific ways in which love is shown. How are you doing at loving the brethren?

Caterpillars and Butterflies

2 Corinthians 5:17; 3:18; Romans 12:2

Introduction:

Are you tired of being what you are? Are you tired of doing what you do? Do you wish you could break away from what things have been? Do you wish you could be different? There is hope! You can change!

I. **The Potential for Change (2 Cor. 5:17)**
   A. Something dramatic takes place at conversion
      1. It is couched in strong words: new birth, new creation, new nature
      2. It is obviously designed to communicate something dynamic
   B. Something is received at the time of conversion:
      1. A new nature—even though the old nature is still present
      2. A new potential—things do not have to be the same anymore
   C. Practical observation gives perspective
      1. This dramatic change is potential
      2. It still doesn't seem to have much effect on many

II. **The Process of Change (2 Cor. 3:18)**
   A. Salvation provides potential; a process achieves the reality
   B. The process described:
      1. With unveiled faces—in contrast to the Old Testament where things were seen less clearly
      2. See the reflection of the glory of the Lord—this is seen in Christ, the Word, nature
      3. By looking at that reflected glory we are changed
      4. As we are changed (metamorphosized) we become more like Him
      5. The change: from the glory of salvation to the glory when we see Him
      6. The Holy Spirit is the agent of this change
   C. What it all means
      1. We can be, are to be, changed
      2. There is a pattern for this change—into what God wants us to be like
      3. This change takes place as we focus on Him through the Word, etc.

4. This change involves a process
5. The Holy Spirit works this change in us

III. The Participation of Change (Rom. 12:2)
A. "Be ye transformed"—this tells us something we are to do
B. This change comes through the "renewing" of our minds
   1. It has to do with a change in our thinking
   2. We have to think along different lines—and in different ways
C. New thinking is necessary
   1. I need to change
   2. I can change—God has provided for it
   3. I must change
   4. I will change
D. This change comes through:
   1. Bible study
   2. Meditation on studied Scripture
   3. Prayer
   4. Simple obedience

Conclusion:
Are you tired of things the way they are? Change is possible! Isn't it time the caterpillar became a butterfly.

Besetting Sins

Ephesians 4:25–32

". . . let us lay aside every weight, and the sin which doth so easily beset us, and let us run with patience the race that is set before us" (Heb. 12:1). Why do we allow "besetting sins" to beset us?

I. **The Issue of Besetting Sin**
   A. The Bible doesn't use the term—it comes from this passage
   B. This is a concept common to experience
      1. Most everyone has a sin that is "besetting"
      2. It is the matter that we struggle with, that comes to mind, that tends to dominate life, that we think of during invitations

II. **The Identification of Besetting Sin**
   A. What we usually think of:
      1. Immorality
      2. Blasphemy
      3. Smoking or drinking
   B. What it usually is—something in the area of this passage:
      1. These are mostly "dispositional sins"
         a. Many have a sour, angry, argumentative, ugly disposition
         b. Others have a problem with the tongue
         c. Still others struggle with outbursts of temper, etc.
      2. These are the sins that keep the majority of Christians from being what God would have them to be

III. **The Involvements of Besetting Sin: Why can't we get on top of these?**
   A. Habit
      1. These were the means of getting our way in childhood or even in later life
      2. They have become unconscious responses
   B. Ignorance
      1. We don't even know that we have a problem
      2. This is an outgrowth of habit
   C. Denial
      1. "I don't really have a problem with . . ." (this is the problem of the alcoholic)

2. You can't conquer a problem that you won't admit you have
D. Disagreement
   1. "I don't think this is that serious a matter"
   2. "I don't agree with the Bible on this so I don't have to obey"
   3. "My situation is different"
E. Comparison
   1. "My case isn't really that bad"
   2. "I'm not nearly as bad on this as _____"
F. Rationalization
   1. "I have a good reason—just cause—for my attitudes and actions"
   2. "If you knew _____, then you'd agree that my case is different"

Conclusion:

We must view the things listed here as sin because they are all evidences of what we should put off. We have allowed external sins to dominate our thinking to the point that we have missed the internal sins of the Spirit. God wants us to change, to become more Christlike, and these things keep us from achieving that goal.

Love, Look Away

Philippians 2:4

Introduction:

There were problems in the Philippian church. From the context, one of them appears to have been excessive concern with self. Paul speaks to the problem, saying, "Love looks away."

I. **The Attitude to Be Avoided**
   A. Self-centeredness
   B. Self-centeredness is avoided by a focus on others

II. **The Approach to Be Taken: it all relates to "one another"**
   A. Prefer one another (Rom. 12:10)
      1. "To lead the way in showing value"
      2. It means honoring by genuinely valuing
   B. Receive one another (Rom. 15:7)
      1. "Grant access to one's heart"
      2. We can accept a person without accepting what he has done
   C. Admonish one another (Rom. 15:14)
      1. "Confront, warn, instruct"
      2. This involves individual believers who are able to help each other
   D. Serve one another (Gal. 5:13)
      1. "To act as a servant, bondslave toward each other"
      2. This requires some difficult things and must be voluntary to be meaningful
   E. Forbear one another (Eph. 4:2)
      1. "To suffer or bear with, endure"
      2. It is putting up with faults, weaknesses
   F. Be kind to one another (Eph. 4:32)
      1. "Mild, pleasant, courteous" as opposed to sharp, harsh, bitter
      2. This involves some element of benevolence
   G. Forgive one another (Col. 3:13)
      1. "To pardon, to restore one to another"
      2. We are to do so even as God for Christ's sake: freely, generously, wholeheartedly, spontaneously, eagerly
   H. Teaching one another (Col. 3:16)
      1. "To hold discourse with so as to instruct"
      2. We should re-punctuate the passage for the best sense

I. Comfort one another (1 Thess. 4:18)
    1. "Go to one's side and feel along with"
    2. This means to encourage, to give added strength to courage
J. Edify one another (1 Thess. 5:11)
    1. "To build up on a foundation"
    2. This means to promote growth of any kind
K. Exhort one another (Heb. 3:13)
    1. "To challenge, call to better performance"
    2. This involves earnest urging
L. Consider one another (Heb. 10:24)
    1. "To fix one's eyes upon, to pay attention to"
    2. This involves trying to see how we can best help someone

III. **The Alternative to Be Rejected**
    A. Self-centeredness is a continual problem
        1. It makes us unpleasant
        2. It skewers our own perceptions
        3. It makes us disobedient
    B. Beyond that, we are to love our neighbor as ourselves
        1. We give serious attention to loving God, but not to this
        2. Following these directions will help us fulfill the task
        3. A focus on others will take the focus off self

Conclusion:
"The shadow of self lies across everything else. Self-worship makes a man prejudiced in holding his own opinions and bigoted in rejecting those of other men." "[Self-centeredness feels] no grief at another's trouble; no pleasure in another's joy." If we are not careful, "Self-will becomes the predominating energy, and self-seeking the prevailing motive."

What's Going On?

Philippians 2:12–13

Introduction:

Is it a good thing to ask, "What is God doing in your life?" Is this a proper question or is it based on some subjective idea? Does God really work in our lives? If He does, what does He do there?

I. **A Challenging Commandment: "Work out your own salvation . . ."**
   - A. This does not refer to salvation from sin
   - B. The meaning is really quite clear:
     1. Keep on working out—developing to the fullest
     2. Your own salvation—the implications of your salvation

II. **An Accompanying Attitude: ". . . with fear and trembling . . ."**
   - A. This means with awe and humility
   - B. The reasons for such an attitude:
     1. The very fact God has saved us should produce awe
     2. The very fact that it is God who saved us should produce humility
     3. The enormous implications of salvation should produce both awe and humility

III. **A Reassuring Reason: "It is God that worketh in you . . ."**
   - A. God does work in us
     1. We are not required to "go it alone"
     2. He does so through the indwelling Holy Spirit
     3. He uses various means in His work
        - a. The Bible
        - b. Other people
        - c. Circumstances
   - B. God does not act instead of us—He works in us
   - C. God does not compel or force us against our wills
     1. Our resistance slows or suspends His work
     2. Our resistance always costs us something

IV. **A Powerful Purpose: ". . . both to will and to do of His own good pleasure"**
   - A. God always has a purpose for what He does in us
     1. That purpose is to conform us to the image of His Son
     2. This is actually what we call sanctification

B. What God does in us
    1. He brings conviction of sin
    2. He helps us see the need of repentance
    3. He enables us to overcome sin
    4. He strengthens us to break with evil influences
    5. He challenges us to give up our evil thoughts
    6. He motivates us to live different lives
    7. He enlightens our minds with truth
    8. He builds our character
    9. He strengthens our relationship with Him
    10. He makes us like He would have us to be
C. God's working in us is always in support of His purposes and in accord with His will as revealed in His Word
    1. God's purposes for us are always good
    2. God takes a long-range view of good

Conclusion:

It is a valid question: What's God doing in your life? It ought to be sharpened: What's God doing in your life right now? God is continually working in us so that the implications of salvation can be fully developed in us. Are you resisting His work? ("The more you cooperate, the less time this will take.") We ought to approach God's working in us with awe and humility.

God's Filling Station

Philippians 4:10–19

Introduction:

Our needs are constant and demanding, but God has promised to supply them all. It is important, however, that we understand what He has actually promised us in verses such as Philippians 4:19.

I. **This Supply Has a Context**
   - A. The connection of the verse
     1. Some want to attach it to verse 20
     2. It is only logical to attach it to verses 10–18
   - B. The creation of the need
     1. The need he was discussing may have arisen from their giving
     2. They certainly had given out of need
   - C. The confines of the need
     1. This surely speaks of a need created by doing right
     2. This does not cover carelessness or profligacy

II. **This Supply Reveals Abundance**
   - A. "Supply"
     1. This means to make full, fill up, "fill to the full"
     2. The idea of God's filling station comes in here
   - B. "My God"
     1. This is a personal expression on Paul's part
     2. The source of our subsistence, "God is our source"
   - C. "Gloriously supply"
     1. "Gloriously" modifies the verb "to supply"
     2. God supplies in a glorious manner (to bring glory to Himself)
   - D. "Riches"
     1. Wealth, abundance, plenitude
     2. This stresses the inexhaustible nature of supply
   - E. "According to"
     1. He does not supply "out of"
     2. He supplies "in accord with," and "in proportion to" (His giving does not diminish the supply in any way)

III. This Supply Involves Restrictions

A. The condition of the context
  1. This is guaranteed only to those meeting the needs of others or (cf. v. 17)
  2. This is guaranteed to those with needs arising out of right actions

B. The condition of God's definition
  1. It has to do with God's definition of "need"
  2. Our financial needs are usually the least of our needs

C. The condition of the silence of the text—it contains no reference to:
  1. When the need will be met
  2. With what the need will be met
  3. How the need will be met

D. The condition of "in Christ Jesus"
  1. The promise is extended only to those who are in Him
  2. He meets the promise to those who are in Him

Conclusion:

God supplies all our needs. He supplies our needs abundantly. He supplies our needs as He sees fit when we are doing right. Isn't it interesting that two great, generally applicable principles of God's Word (vv. 13 and 19) arise out of a section on giving?

Does God Really Supply All Our Needs?
Philippians 4:14–19

Introduction:
Many struggle with questions regarding God's supply in spite of the clear statement of verse 19 of our text. Let's look at what the Word really says:

I. **A Straightforward Expression**
   A. It is unconditional
      1. There are no obvious conditions here
      2. "I would hate to be in a position to need His supply if I had not been meeting my obligations to the Lord and had been selfish in regard to the needs of others"
   B. It is unlimited
      1. It identifies God as making the provision
      2. It speaks of "all" your needs
      3. It bases everything on God's riches in glory
      4. It involves Jesus
   C. It is unspecified
      1. It does not say exactly what He will do
      2. It does not say how He will do it
      3. It does not say when He will do it

II. **A Strange Experience**
   A. We have all been through experiences in which it appears our needs have not been met
   B. We have all been through experiences in which our needs have been met but not as or when we thought they should be
   C. The question comes to mind, Does God really meet all our needs?

III. **A Scriptural Explanation: What about the times when it appears He does not do so?**
   A. Our need was not really a need
      1. We become accustomed to a specific lifestyle
      2. The truth is that God actually provides many of our wants
   B. It is a matter of timing
      1. The story of Joseph is most instructive
      2. God always has His reasons for His timing
   C. The need is supplied but not in the way you wanted it to be

1. The story of Israel in the wilderness (He gave them what they needed, when they needed it, in ways of His choosing rather than theirs, in ways at times not even visible, in ways designed to test them, in ways also designed to humble them)
2. God knows best how to supply our needs

D. The need is not our greatest need
   1. We have many needs, but we see the temporal, physical as the most important; God sees our spiritual needs as greatest
   2. God may not supply one need because that need is being used in the process of meeting another more important one

E. Meeting the need the way we want it, in the time we want would not bring Him ultimate glory
   1. The meeting of needs is a means of His glorification
   2. He usually does things so as to bring glory to Himself ahead of bringing comfort to us

Conclusion:

All our needs are occasions for blessing and glory. He does meet need; don't give up. He does promise to meet one need every time, and that is the need for salvation.

A Sure Thing

Philippians 4:19

Introduction:
There are very few "sure things," but there are things you can be sure of, however, such things as the promises of God. There is a great one here:

I. **The Need: "... all your needs ..."**
    A. We have two basic kinds of needs
        1. Material/temporal/physical
        2. Spiritual
    B. We have a wrong focus regarding needs
        1. All temporal needs boil down to three (food, clothing, shelter); spiritual needs are almost infinite (pardon, strength, instruction, comfort, quickening, etc.) "We are just a bag of wants and a heap of infirmities."—Spurgeon
        2. We think much of temporal and little of spiritual needs
            a. This is shown by our prayer habits
            b. This is shown by our ingratitudes
    C. Notice that it is "all" our needs that are covered

II. **The Supply: "... shall supply ..."**
    A. "My God will fill to the full all your need"
        1. This is indication of provision
        2. This is indication of complete provision
    B. A statement of fact
        1. "God shall supply"
        2. Remember that it is needs that He will supply
    C. This should affect our thinking
        1. If we don't get it, did we need it?
        2. The more genuine the needs, the more full the supply

III. **The Source: "My God ..."**
    A. This directs us to the God of heaven
        1. It brings His attributes into view
        2. It connects us to His ultimate power
    B. Notice the personal pronoun *my*
        1. We have access to the God of Paul and all other Bible characters
        2. This drives us back to Scriptures in times of need

IV. **The Resources: "... according to His riches in glory"**
   A. There are infinite resources involved
      1. "He owns the cattle ..."
      2. In Him are hid all the riches of the wisdom and knowledge of God
   B. God possess resources for miracles but He usually works according to His promises—we sometimes see His hand moving; other times simply get to know it has moved

V. **The Connection: "... by Christ Jesus"**
   A. God's promise to supply all our needs is tied to Christ
      1. He must be part of the equation
      2. This becomes a limited promise
   B. The promise is limited to those who know Jesus Christ as Savior
      1. He may supply the needs of others
      2. He will supply the needs of His own

Conclusion:

God has promised to supply all our needs. We can count on that promise even though we may not be able to understand the details. There is a strong statement that is completely true: the more you invest in the work of the Lord, in supporting His servants, in meeting the needs of the needy, the more this will be a "sure thing" in your life.

An Alternate Focus

1 Timothy 6:11–16

Introduction:
What is materialism? The Christian view: a focus on material things to the exclusion of or in competition with a spiritual emphasis. Who is a materialist? Just about everyone! There is an alternative, says Paul.

I. **Focus on Spiritual Values (v. 11)**
    A. The negative
        1. "Flee"—turn away from
        2. "These things"—this primarily relates to what he has just said
        3. "Man of God"—anyone who belongs to God
    B. The positive
        1. "Follow after"—pursue, diligently seek
        2. The qualities
            a. "Righteousness"—general term for right heart
            b. "Godliness"—that which is like God
            c. "Faith, love, patience, meekness": fruit of the Spirit
        3. It is putting a focus on spiritual verities as priorities and goals

II. **Focus on Your Life Purposes (v. 12)**
    A. Two commands:
        1. "Fight the good fight"—this is involved with the faith
        2. "Lay hold on eternal life"—that to which you were called
    B. Live in accord with what you have already shown everyone
    C. The whole point is to remember the purpose of your life and live in accord with it

III. **Focus on Future Realities (vv. 13–14)**
    A. Note the emphasis of the verses: "I give thee charge . . . keep this commandment . . . until the appearing of the Lord Jesus Christ"
        1. The emphasis is on the second coming
        2. This brings an eternal dimension into the picture
    B. Note the details of the verses
        1. The charge is given in the sight of God—the God

who quickeneth all things

    2. The charge is also given in the sight of Christ—the Christ who had a good confession before Pilate

    3. The commandment is to be kept without spot and unrebukable

  C. The point of the verses is to introduce the theme of the future

    1. This life is not all there is

    2. The next life is what really matters

IV. Focus on the Character of God (vv. 15–16)

  A. This is a great doctrinal statement

    1. It was not, however, designed for that purpose

    2. It was actually designed to point up what he is saying about the alternatives to materialism

  B. It introduces the idea of God

    1. It tells us much about God

    2. It emphasizes His power and majesty

  C. It stresses that we don't have to be materialists

    1. We have plenty without that

    2. Our God is able to take care of everything without our becoming involved in materialism

Conclusion:

We all have that materialism within. Paul tells Timothy—and us—to resist it and the way to do so lies in a proper focus. Materialism is a matter of your focus, and it is best conquered by a change in that focus.

What to Do with What You've Got

1 Timothy 6:17–19

Introduction:
The Bible has much to say about money. It speaks about desiring it, and it speaks to those who have it. Don't stop listening—there is something for you here.

I.   **The Relativity of Riches (v. 17a)**
  A.   "Rich in terms of this present age"
    1.   We see riches in man's terms
    2.   God sees riches in entirely different terms
  B.   This shows us that riches are always relative
    1.   To be really rich is always to have slightly more than we already have
    2.   But we are richer than almost anyone on earth

II.   **Warnings for the Wealthy (v. 17b): to each one of us**
  A.   Don't be snobbish
    1.   "Be not highminded"—from two words: lofty and think
    2.   Beware of "pride of purse"
  B.   Don't be smug
    1.   "Nor trust in the uncertainty of riches"
    2.   Don't find security in what you have

III.   **Principles of Prosperity (vv. 17c–18)**
  A.   Set your hope on God
    1.   A matter of focus—God should be that focus
    2.   God is the perfect point of focus
      a.   He gives all things
      b.   He gives us all things
      c.   He gives us all things richly
      d.   He gives us all things richly to be enjoyed (it is not wrong to have things so long as the focus is right)
  B.   Work that which is good
    1.   Make work of doing good
    2.   The same word is used of God in Acts 14:17
  C.   Be rich in honorable deeds
    1.   Abound in things that are honorable
    2.   Make a collection of honorable acts—do so many honorable things that they are hard to discern
  D.   Be quick to recognize needs

1. This word contains the idea of awareness of the needs of others
2. The English word "generosity" fits in well
   E. Be willing to give what you have
   1. Be ready and willing to share with others what you have
   2. This puts the focus where it belongs

IV. The Intelligence of Investment (v. 19)
   A. Provision for the future
   1. "Laying up in store for themselves"—investing
   2. "A good foundation"—in contrast to the shaky foundation provided by riches
   3. "Against the time to come"—the future, especially the judgment seat of Christ
   B. Performance for the present
   1. "That they may hold on to what is really life"
   2. The idea is that the person who learns how to handle riches is the only person who really understands what life is all about

Conclusion:

The underlying biblical philosophy: Old Testament saints showed their wealth by possession; New Testament saints by their giving. God—especially in the New Testament—shows interest in giving, not in having. Until you have learned to give, you have not learned what life is all about. Never forget that it is ". . . God, who giveth us richly all things to enjoy."

Procrastination

Hebrews 3:7–19; 4:7

Introduction:

Someone has said, "Never do today what you can put off until tomorrow because tomorrow you may not have to do it." This is a tongue-in-cheek statement that is tragically true. All of us have something of the procrastinator in us, and two questions make it easy to discern when he is operating: "Are you going to do that?" and "When?" The answer to the second question will tell the tale.

I. **Procrastination Is a Helpful Tool**
   A. It keeps us from having to face an issue by continuous postponement
   B. It keeps us from ever having to make a final decision
   C. It avoids having to tell someone "no"
   D. It shields us from having to face the consequences of our decisions or actions
   E. It prevents having to close the door on any options
   F. But indecision itself is a decision

II. **Procrastination Makes Significant Statements: when you say "later" you are actually saying something else as well**
   A. This matter isn't that important
   B. This matter really doesn't make any difference
   C. There's plenty of time to take care of this matter
   D. There are other things that are way more important than this
   E. We are really saying: someone or something is more important to me

III. **Procrastination (Spiritually) Is Usually Caused By**
   A. Fear of failure
      1. We are afraid we won't be able to hold out, stay with it, keep a commitment, hang in
      2. This fails to take into account God's willingness to help
   B. Fear of difficulty
      1. We are afraid that something will be too hard to do
      2. This fails to take into account God's enabling

C. Fear of insufficient results
   1. We fear boredom after taking some step
   2. This fails to take into account God's ability to satisfy and even energize

IV. **Procrastination Can Be Fatal (cf. Acts 24:24–27)**
   A. Paul was in trouble because of a riot in Jerusalem
      1. He claims the benefits of Roman citizenship
      2. He gets caught in that Roman legal system
   B. Felix is a Roman politician and a typical one
      1. He wants a bribe
      2. He wants to be popular
   C. Paul and Felix interact—drawn out by this politicism
      1. Paul preaches to him and his wife (his third?)
      2. He is obviously moved by the message
   D. There is no indication Felix ever responded—he might as well not have heard the message, because it is worse to hear and not act ("delay, the ultimate form of denial")

Conclusion:
   The present is the only time you have to work with. The past is gone and can't be reclaimed, and the future is not yet here and can't be guaranteed. What you would do, you should do now. What is it you should do? "Life is not a dress rehearsal."

Timely Help

Hebrews 4:16

Introduction:
God encourages His people to pray, and He also promises results when they do so.

I. **An Open Invitation: God encourages us to pray**
   A. The destination—". . . the throne of grace . . ."
   B. The invitation—"Let us . . . come . . ."
   C. The manner—". . . boldly . . ."
   D. The basis—". . . therefore . . ."
      1. We have a sure Word from God (v. 12)
      2. We have a God who already knows our needs (v. 13)
      3. We have a Great High Priest for an advocate (v. 14)
      4. Our Advocate is a knowledgeable representative (v. 15)

II. **A Clear Priority**
   A. The most common thing
      1. The vast majority of our prayer is for the supply of temporal needs and wants
      2. We pray as we do because we think as we do
   B. The most important thing
      1. This phrase deals with spiritual realities
      2. It mentions great theological concepts
      3. It actually includes temporal supply, but it puts the emphasis first on spiritual needs

III. **An Abundant Supply**
   A. Definition
      1. Mercy: That aspect of God's character that takes pity on man and doesn't give him what he actually deserves
      2. Grace: That aspect of God's character that looks to man's need and gives him something that he doesn't deserve
   B. Distinction
      1. We "receive" mercy—"obtain" has too much of effort or merit in it
      2. We "find" grace—it is there, and we just come upon it

C. Comprehensiveness
   1. Mercy covers not getting the things we deserve
   2. Grace includes receiving everything we need

IV. A Specific Timeliness
   A. For every time—there are multitudinous times of need
      1. When pressed by temptation
      2. When beset by danger
      3. When assailed by doubt
      4. When we "stand in slippery places"
      5. When suffering bodily affliction
      6. When simply "short of supplies"
   B. Just in time—every time
      1. "Time of need"—just when the need arises
      2. His arrival is always "timely"

Conclusion:
What more could you need? What more could you ask? What more could He give?

God's Track Team

Hebrews 12:1–3

Introduction:

Many runners enter a race, but only one wins the prize. Run to win!

I. **Let Us Run the Race**
- A. Note the metaphor: a race involves effort and pain
- B. Note the fixed menu: "that is set before us"—we don't get to choose the course, and we don't have the option of quitting
- C. Note the manner: you will run the race!—the only question is how will you run it?—what is recommended is "steadfast endurance, perseverance"

II. **Let Us See the Witnesses: they do not observe us; they bear witness to us**
- A. Abel: things don't always go well
- B. Enoch: it pays to walk with God
- C. Noah: He will surely keep you through the storm
- D. Abraham: you're never too old for God's purposes
- E. Joseph: trials only come to make you strong
- F. Moses: God's way is the best way
- G. Joshua: "not by might nor by power"

III. **Let Us Lay Aside the Weight**
- A. That which hinders our running—to be hooked or attached by a hook
- B. That which entangles us
  1. Sins of our natural disposition
  2. Sins from the past
  3. Sins to which we are exposed
  4. Sins from our weakness of character
- C. All external and internal hindrances, care and burdens, etc.

IV. **Let Us Look to Jesus—Our Example**
- A. A perfect example
  1. "Author"—initiator: He is the One who invented faith
  2. "Finisher"—completer: He is the "end all" of faith
- B. A practical example
  1. He endured the cross

    2. He had mixed emotions: joy/shame

    3. He looked beyond the shame to the joy

V.   A Perfect Example

    A. He has succeeded

    B. He has received the reward as forerunner of all else who will receive the reward

Conclusion:

Run the race—hear the witnesses—lay aside the weights—keep looking unto Jesus. "The best means of leading a faithful Christian life, amidst the opposition we may encounter, is to keep the eyes steadily fixed on the Savior."

Roots

Hebrews 12:15

Introduction:

What is the most common sin among Christians? Bitterness would have to rank among the most common, and it is one of the most damaging.

I. **The Character of Bitterness**
   A. Defined: strong, negative, internal feelings that have become settled in regard to something or someone
   B. It may be directed in one of three directions:
      1. Toward God
      2. Toward circumstances
      3. Toward another person

II. **The Cause of Bitterness**
   A. Failure to come to terms with the God-allowed circumstances of life
   B. Failure to deal with the issues of life
   C. Failure to follow biblically-presented procedures regarding life's relationships

III. **The Curse of Bitterness**
   A. It produces outbursts
      1. Pent-up emotions often escape
      2. This explains some incredible outbursts
   B. It grieves the Holy Spirit (Eph. 4:30)
      1. The Holy Spirit has the function of peace and unity
      2. It makes an unpleasant environment for Him
   C. It has effects on others ("and thereby many be defiled")
      1. It has an element of contagion
      2. There is a degree to which it changes us
      3. It causes us to make foolish decisions
   D. We filter all of life through it
      1. We see bad where none exists
      2. We fail to see that which is good
   E. It creates a climate for constant misinterpretation
      1. We see problems where none exist
      2. We misunderstand people's motives, etc.

IV. **The Cure for Bitterness**
   A. Forgiveness:
      1. Which involves forgiving from the heart
      2. Granting forgiveness where asked

B. Confrontation
   1. Where we have offended (Matt. 5:23–24)
   2. Where we have been offended (Matt. 18:15ff)
   3. Where we have been mistreated (Rom. 12:17–21)
C. Acceptance (2 Cor. 12:7–10)
   1. If anyone could be bitter, how about Paul?
   2. Paul was hindered in his service
   3. He exemplifies more than passive acceptance—". . . will I rather glory in my infirmities . . ."

Conclusion:

If you don't deal with the bitterness, the bitterness will deal with you.

Purify Yourself?

1 Peter 1:22–25

Introduction:

There is much confusion about sanctification. In practice, most Christians believe it is something that "just happens," but biblical teaching is really different. Peter makes an unusual statement here: "Seeing ye have purified your souls . . ." What does he mean by that? Can you really purify your own soul?

I. To What Does the Statement Refer?
   A. It obviously refers to salvation—note the past tense of the verb and the entire context of the passage
   B. It also refers to sanctification—the perfect construct of the verb allows this—"You have purified—and are purifying—yourselves"

II. What Does the Statement Mean?
   A. We are active participants in our own purification
   B. Explanation—we become involved in our own salvation—it is not something that just happens to us without our participation, and we are deeply involved in our own sanctification

III. How Does One Do This?
   A. "In obeying the truth"
      1. "Through or by means of"
      2. Obedience becomes the means of purification
   B. "The truth" here is contained in the Word
      1. This is mentioned twice in the passage
      2. The Word is the means of salvation and sanctification
   C. Summary: We play a part in our salvation and our sanctification, and that part is obedience to the truth as it is in the Word of God

IV. What Is Necessary to Do This?
   A. "Through the Spirit"
      1. By means of the Holy Spirit
      2. With the help, aid, assistance of the Holy Spirit
   B. We play a role, but it is impossible without the work of the Holy Spirit
      1. Salvation is not totally passive
      2. Sanctification is not at all passive, but it is impossible without the Holy Spirit

V. In What Does This Result?
A. "Unto unfeigned love of the brethren"
  1. Salvation and sanctification result in brotherly love
  2. It takes that change to get us away from natural tendencies
B. Note that the love is to be "unfeigned"
  1. "Without hypocrisy"
  2. To do anything "unfeigned" takes continual self-examination

VI. Is This Ever Perfect or Permanent?
A. Note the repetition of the phrase—"see that ye love one another . . ."
  1. This is not an empty repetition
  2. Salvation and sanctification provide for the possibility; now it is up to us to carry it out
B. We are running against the old nature
  1. It takes constant effort to keep us going
  2. Peter adds "fervently"—a strong word indicating an expenditure of effort

VII. On What Is This All Based?
A. The fact that the Word of God is permanently enduring
  1. There is no danger of failure with the Word
  2. There is no danger of change with the Word
B. The stress of both salvation and sanctification is the Word of God
  1. Salvation does not occur apart from the Word
  2. Sanctification does not occur apart from deliberate obedience to the Word of God

Conclusion:
Sanctification is not just a doctrine to be learned, but a practice to be pursued.

Goal: To Grow

1 Peter 2:1–3

Introduction:

There is much emphasis on church growth today. Such growth is important, but there is other growth just as important and that is spiritual growth.

I. **The Goal: Spiritual Growth (v. 2)**
   A. Growth itself is the goal
      1. The journey, not the destination is in view
      2. Growth is a sure proof of life
   B. There are comparisons with natural growth
      1. It is natural for life to progress
      2. Growth should affect all areas of life
   C. This contrasts with natural growth
      1. It is not spontaneous
      2. It is optional
      3. It is terminable
   D. There are lessons to be learned
      1. It is continuous (never arriving)
      2. It is universal (everyone needs it)
      3. It is constant (necessary all the time, at a constant rate)

II. **The Means: The Word of God (vv. 1–2)**
   A. The objective Word
      1. "Sincere"—unadulterated
      2. "Milk"—likened to mother's milk
      3. "Desire"—long for, earnestly seek (read, know, study, hear)
      4. Application, not absorption is important
      5. There is no growth apart from the Word
   B. There are things to be laid aside—put off, like a garment
      1. "Malice"—general term for evil in all its forms
      2. "Guile"—deceit—deliberate attempt to mislead by lies
      3. "Hypocrisies"—pretending to be other than what one is
      4. "Envies"—not wanting others to have what they have
      5. "Evil speakings"—running down each other

III. **The Impetus: Your Spiritual Experience (v. 3)**
   A. Two spiritual experiences in view
      1. If you have tasted of His grace—if you have known saving grace
      2. If you have tasted of His graciousness—if you have known something of His working in your life
   B. Knowing Him and how He works should be an impetus to the kind of growth that involves coming to know Him better
      1. If you've ever tasked something good . . .
      2. Lack of spiritual appetite usually stems from lack of spiritual experience or lack of exposure to Scripture

Conclusion:
   "Growth in grace is a pilgrimage to be trod with bleeding feet." Once you have really tasted what He is like, how can you keep from going on in and with Him?

The Reverend Everybody
1 Peter 4:10

Introduction:
There is a big stress today on the idea that everyone is a minister. This is a thoroughly biblical stress. "Every man has some gift; no man has all. So every man must minister."

I. **A Possession**
   A. The gift is always received
      1. It is not something one earns
      2. It can and should be developed, but it is received
   B. The gift comes at conversion
      1. It may be a special donation at that time
      2. It may merely be the spiritual energizing of a natural gift
   C. The gift is anything I have that my brothers lack
      1. It is anything by which one can benefit another
      2. It is all the gifts and graces by which one can help another

II. **Its Purpose**
   A. To minister is to serve
      1. It comes from a word that means "lowly service"
      2. The idea is that of a server in a restaurant
   B. To minister is to help others
      1. Wherever there is a need, there is an opportunity
      2. The Samaritan understood ministry

III. **Its Practice**
   A. A good steward is "a responsible slave"
      1. He receives what he has (stewardship does not involve one's own things)
      2. What he has belongs to another
      3. He is to use what he has since God has given him enough to meet all his needs (if there are unmet needs, it may mean that someone is not functioning)
      4. He is to be accountable for what he has
   B. His stewardship is of God's appointment
      1. "Manifold" = plentiful, varied
      2. "Grace" = God's free gifts

IV. **Its Practice**
   A. It is totally comprehensive
      1. "Every man" is involved

     2. Since every man has the gift, every man is required to participate (there is no way to "sit this one out")
- B. It is completely individual
  1. This is not a matter for "the church"
  2. This is a matter for which we will give account

Conclusion:

"The gifts of grace . . . are talents (or abilities) entrusted to individual Christians for the good of the whole church. Those who have them must use them to minister to the wants (needs) of others."

"All gifts are trusts . . . no Christian gets his natural endowments . . . material possessions . . . spiritual graces for himself alone."

Submission and Humility

1 Peter 5:5–7

Introduction:

Note that there are two key issues in this passage: 1) Submit: voluntarily place yourself under the authority of another. 2) Be humble: "low-lying, not rising far above the ground"; have a deep sense of your own littleness.

I. **The Exhortation (v. 5): "Submit yourselves . . ."**
    A. Younger to older
        1. There is no reference to church offices here
        2. This simply has to do with younger people submitting to older people
    B. Everyone to everyone
        1. There is some question about the text here but no real problem (Eph. 5:21)
        2. This speaks of a general mind-set (Phil. 2:1–4)
        3. It involves each one looking for opportunities to put others first

II. **The Example (v. 5): "In the same way . . ."**
    A. "Likewise" means "in the same way"
    B. Submission to each other is to be in the same way as the elders submit to their tasks
        1. "Not by constraint"
        2. "Not for filthy lucre"
        3. "Not as being lords over God's heritage"
    C. Just as elders are to submit to a difficult and thankless task, so we all are to do something equally difficult and thankless—submit

III. **The Extension (vv. 5–6)**
    A. Be clothed with humility (v. 5)
        1. "Be clothed"—this is the only use in the New Testament—it comes from a combination of words that indicate an apron knotted around one's garments to indicate slavery
        2. "Clothe yourself"—take care of it yourself
        3. Genuine humility is an identifying mark of true Christianity
    B. Be characterized by humility (v. 6)
        1. "Humble yourselves under the mighty hand of God"—this is an act of the will that involves a proper sense of perspective

2. It is a basic requirement of being clothed with humility—we won't yield to others without this

IV. **The Exaltation (vv. 5–6)**
   A. A present reward (v. 5)
      1. God gives grace to the humble
      2. The arrogant and proud don't need it
   B. A future recognition (v. 6)
      1. Humility will ultimately be exalted
      2. "Due time" leaves the time options with God

V. **The Enablement (v. 7): "All the anxiety of you casting on Him because to Him it matters concerning you"**
   A. Contextual connection
      1. There is a large measure of stress involved in submission
      2. There are anxieties in humbling one's self
   B. Challenge
      1. "Cast"—roll, toss, heap
      2. "All your care"—very inclusive
   C. Concern—"it matters to Him about you"
      1. Everything about you matters to Him
      2. Things that we encounter while following His will appear to matter to Him in a special way

Conclusion:
"One of the greatest differences in the world is that between the commandments of the Bible and the performance of God's people."